Published by Willow Creek Press, Inc.
P.O. Box 147, Minocqua, Wisconsin 54548
Printed in China

ISBN: 978-1-62343-416-8

Edited by Deborah McKew

Book Design by RavenMark, Inc.

Illustrations by Linda Mirabile (pp. 19, 95, 119) and Shearon Murphy (p. 43)

Maps made with Natural Earth. Free vector and raster map data@naturalearthdata.com

All photographs ©Ginger Poleschook and Daniel Poleschook, Jr., except for the following:

Contributing Photographers:
    Sharon Day/Shutterstock: Grand Tetons, Wyoming (p. 12)
    Cory J. Gregory: Whitefish Point, Michigan (pp. 20-21)
    Airphoto-Jim Wark: Arctic tundra (p. 86)
    jmoor/iStock: Walker Lake, Nevada (p. 110)
    David Clausen: Baja California, Mexico (p. 120)
    Jonathan Fiely: Loon raft (p. 136)

Video Contributors:
    Cinematography by Tim Smith and Jonathan Fiely
    Production by Argali Films

The mission of Biodiversity Research Institute is to assess emerging threats to wildlife and ecosystems through collaborative research and to use scientific findings to advance environmental awareness and inform decision makers.

The mission of the Ricketts Conservation Foundation is to support the conservation of wildlife and wilderness areas, and to promote the importance of environmental stewardship as an enduring value.

We would like to thank the Ricketts Conservation Foundation
for their tremendous support of loon conservation at a critical time.
We thank Jeff Fair who has provided us invaluable historical perspective, insight, and
friendship for many years. We thank Deborah McKew and Linda Mirabile for their
talent and dedication toward this project. We also thank Lee Attix and
Iain Stenhouse for their review of the material, and Jim Paruk for technical advice.
We extend our gratitude to the dedicated staff at Biodiversity Research Institute's Center
for Loon Conservation, to our fellow colleagues, field biologists,
and the many volunteers who have been instrumental in the collection of loon data.

And finally, to Taylor and Thomas, our future wildlife biologists,
who waited patiently while we wrote this book.

Contents

In the end, it is this journey of the loon that inspires our conservation; we wish to keep the magic in our lives.

FOREWORD

By Jeff Fair

For a brief period as a young graduate student in wildlife ecology, I held myself under the impressions that all biology was hard science and that I was in graduate school in order to become a fully fledged Ph.D. research biologist—white coat, university sinecure, statistical confidence intervals and all. I had no idea at the time that I was there primarily to meet a number of long-time mentors and to refine—or redefine—my own journey in life.

Some of that redefinition occurred early on, in particular one weekend that first autumn. Two of my graduate-student comrades had invited me to join them on a camping foray up into northern New Hampshire on the shores of Umbagog Lake. North being my direction already, I arranged to meet them by canoe at a lakeside wilderness campsite called Moll's Rock. Our rock (and the sweet, grassy field behind it) was named for an Abenaki woman whom the early white men thereabouts called Molly Molasses for her fondness of the sweet syrup. She had been the wife of the last of the Abenaki band in those parts, a man called Chief Metallak, and when she died, legend was, she was buried here on Umbagog under Moll's Rock.

I crawled into my old sleeping bag in my cheap tent (J.C. Penney's, $19.95) out there over Moll's grave, my ripstop floor ruffled for a while by the meadow voles who'd camped there before I had. When they finally quieted and I was just falling asleep, the wailing of ancient native spirits began. Lord. Haunting, crazy-wild spirits, screaming and laughing unexpectedly loud—not from above but from quite near me, down by the lake, filling the boreal night with funereal threats and foreboding and mystery. And music.

I'd read about loons, their voices symbolizing that same wild North that I so aspired to, but I'd never heard them before. That night they routed my dreams with the reality of a wilder life, calling in from just outside the zipper of my little blue tent, there above Moll's bones and under the starry New Hampshire sky. In a way, I had met my future. I'd heard my calling. The journey northward that I'd longed for had now begun. And not by science, but rather by spirit.

Less than four years later I would spend the summer surveying and studying the sources of those same frightening sounds, there on Umbagog. And for the next 36 years I would continue to follow and observe and study loons, in various manners and among a wonderful array of colleagues. I was inspired to forego the Ph.D. and remain in the field, as we call it, meaning under the open skies and upon the open water of loon country. It seemed worth it to me then, as it does now, to escape the complexities and to enjoy and celebrate the real world with a simpler, more comprehensive analysis.

The Common Loon's journey may be described in several ways. It might be its journey through the millennia of evolutionary time from the days of the flightless, diving birds of the Cretaceous Period to today's graceful *Gavia immer*. And of course, it could be the modern loon's annual peregrinations between winter and breeding habitats that comprise the framework of its natural history through the seasons and which are explained and illustrated so capably by the text and photographs on the pages that follow. But here I'd like to explore another kind of journey that the loon has made hand-in-wing with us humans—a journey through the human psyche across the ages.

Long ago, early humans around the northern hemisphere honored the loon's voice with magical and near god-like qualities. Legends arose—some of them still repeated today—of the loon as creator, as healer, as savior, a spirit-voice of deceased warriors.

Early on, too, the loon represented food for the Native hunter and insulated waterproof skin for parkas, food storage, even pouches to keep cartridges dry. As a fish eater, the loon was later disparaged by fishermen, and killed as a predator well into the last century by fishermen. The loon was even shot for sport from the boats on Northeastern lakes during that era between the development of accurate firepower and the advent of the conservation ethic.

But then the conservation era dawned, and loons were studied and described scientifically—quite simply at first—and later became recognized as barometers of the aquatic environment. The indiscriminant shooting was made illegal, and more complex research evolved to answer the questions necessary to conserve the loons and protect their journeys. We tried to voiceprint them by recording their yodels; later we color-banded them to recognize individuals. We began to take blood and feather samples to measure the poisons in their bodies and to peek into their genes; we followed some of their journeys by satellite.

There have been times when I've feared that as a biologist I'd become too caught up in the science and forgotten the joy of my own journey. That occurred once years ago when we were recording loon yodels. I'd been out all day by canoe, and had just recorded a yodel from the Rapid River male on Umbagog that carried 16 repetitions of the final phrase. I'd been very close, and that seemed like some really good *data*.

But back at the camp where I was staying alone, after sundown things seemed to change, and the recording was less important. I felt too alone. It finally occurred to me that my company was the same as my science, out there on the water. So, I took the canoe back out onto the big north bay of the lake and slithered over the center gunnel into the black water, and hung there, one hand on the gunnel and up to my earlobes in Umbagog, under the stars. Eventually, a loon chorus arose, and I received it ("listened" is too weak a verb) at loon level. Seven pairs sang and answered one another: Rapid River was first, then Sunday Cove, Pine Point, Sturtevant, Stag Camp, Leonard Marsh, and Marsh Inlet. The magic of that night overwhelmed the day's recording by twentyfold.

Authors Dave Evers and his wife and partner loon biologist Kate Taylor write in the following pages that, "conservation of these creatures requires careful and considerate documentation of all parts of [their] wild heritage—not simply as a scientific inquiry, but as a human responsibility and as a privilege." I so agree. And, I might add, as a simple human joy, the joy of understanding—if only in a small way—such a wild spirit. But, also the joy in what we do not and sometimes cannot know, in what the loons surprise us with, even the field biologists (and perhaps *mostly* us) who feel rather familiar with the species.

I think of walking out by a lake still mostly ice-covered one morning in April and hearing a tremolo and seeing a loon flying overhead on a reconnaissance flight. Or, suddenly seeing dozens of loons on the lake one autumn day—I mean several dozens, suddenly there and in a long line, like a pearl necklace, diving simultaneously to fish. Or, flying up lake in a fast boat and having a loon suddenly appear in the passing lane, outspeeding a 90 hp Merc. Or, towing a nesting raft into a cove apparently empty of its resident pair, only to have the pair silently surface ten feet away, close enough to hear them breathing, to monitor our progress.

How many times have we searched a cove for hours—no loons—only to motor out of it and hear the tremolo-laughter behind us? Or, watched a loon near our boat in big water where we could see a mile in every direction, and then with one dive, the loon disappears…forever.

Or, that night on Umbagog when we could not manage to capture the Glassby Cove pair and finally shut off our spotlights, and seconds later one of them appeared in the darkness right next to the boat, beside my net, as if giving itself to our research.

It is the loon's journey through the human psyche that intrigues me most. As much as any single loon wings off to the autumn sea only to return to the waters of its origin or recent nesting, so too does the metaphoric loon of both biology and legend journey through the human psyche only to circle home again. From its origins of enchantment and spellbinding fear or fascination, the loon travels into myth, legend, usefulness, food, environmental symbolism, and finally full circle back to its feathered magic in those expressions of its life that enthrall us.

In the end, it is this journey of the loon that inspires our conservation; we wish to keep the magic in our lives. Conservation is but a tool of hope, a necessary part of our own journey back into the romance of the wild.

Lazy Mountain, Alaska
Late winter, 2014

INTRODUCTION

By David Evers and Kate Taylor

On an August evening in 1998, we set out in a canoe to capture loons on a small pond on Mount Desert Island in Maine. We hoped the quiet of night and carefully chosen recordings of loon calls would draw the pair and young chick close. The sky shimmered white with northern lights, mirroring the low spiraling layers of mist that had formed over the water. In the deepest parts of the lake, the air felt cool, turning rich and earthy with stirred sediment as we poled through shallower areas. We moved slowly in the direction of loon calls, noting the flights of bats overhead, their movements curving with the arc of our paddles in the water.

Silently embedded in the scene, we followed the sound of loons into darkened coves, sometimes chasing the sudden slap of water made from a dive in the shadow of our canoe. At dawn, we were forced to quit, the early light exposing both our intent and position. We never saw the pair and their chick that evening.

Although we did not succeed in capturing the loons, we left feeling rewarded. This is the gift of sharing space with loons, and is a reminder of the importance not only of loons, but of the places in which they live. Sigurd Olsen, a naturalist and writer of the North Woods, once wrote of loons as a symbol of wildness, reminding us of our own connection to nature. We have found this to be very true.

This book provides a venue for us to share our experience of loons, allowing the photographs to depict the seasonal cycles that define the life of loons—from their twice yearly migrations, to claiming territories and mates in the spring, through the hatches of summer and fledges of fall, and finally, to the solitude of winter. The images compiled by Ginger and Daniel Poleschook offer a rare opportunity to witness the private moments of loons, all captured with great care and consideration, and chosen for this volume in that same spirit. It is our hope that the images gracefully express why loons have been charted through history in cultural myths and legends, and why they continue to richly characterize the woodland waters and landscape.

THE COMMON LOON—POPULATION AND PLACES

The Common Loon (*Gavia immer*), one of five loon species that exist worldwide, is the only loon species that breeds in the contiguous United States. The closely related Yellow-billed Loon (*G. adamsii*) is a strictly tundra and coastal plain breeding species and is the rarest loon species (around 3,000 individuals in Alaska). Pacific (*G. pacifica*) and Arctic Loons (*G. arctica*) are smaller than the Common Loon. The Pacific Loon is mostly restricted to North America, while the Arctic Loon is primarily a breeding species found in Europe and Asia. Lastly, the Red-throated Loon (*G. stellata*) has the widest range of all loon species and is found across the Northern Hemisphere.

Through monitoring, banding, and satellite tracking, we have gathered critical information on the size and movements of loon breeding populations. An estimated 620,000 loons call North America their summer home, with their numbers growing in the fall to more than 725,000 with the addition of summer's chicks. The core part of the loon's breeding range is in Ontario and Quebec, with other large breeding centers in the Northwest Territories and British Columbia. The largest U.S. breeding populations, with more than 12,000 adults, each occur in both Alaska and Minnesota.

We tend to associate the Common Loon with the North Woods—preferred habitats of clear, deep lakes surrounded by tall spruce and pines. Yet, these loons live widely and in a variety of habitats, including shallow and managed pools, turbid reservoirs, beaver ponds, sphagnum bog lakes, and relatively high elevation lakes. Small populations are also found reaching past the taiga zone, extending across portions of the coastal plains, and in some cases into the tundra of the high Arctic. Here, in the eastern half of North America's tundra, Common Loons nest and raise young on lakes with treeless shorelines.

In winter, the loon's habitat varies just as widely. Loons overwinter along both the Atlantic and Pacific coastlines. On the southern fringes of the winter range, loons occupy coastal shorelines near the arid, cactus-lined shores of Mexico. In the Gulf of Mexico, wintering loons are associated with bays ringed with live oak and Spanish moss.

CONNECTION AND CONSERVATION

As loon biologists, our job is to pursue and publish the results of our work, addressing the needs of loons on a population level. Holding loons in the hand, however, and documenting their individual life histories creates connection, and even kinship. That sense of connection is shared among others who do this work—

our fellow biologists at Biodiversity Research Institute's Center for Loon Conservation who work long hours, in often challenging conditions; our good friend and wildlife biologist Jeff Fair, who has spent more time "under the open skies" with loons than anyone else we know; Maine wildlife biologist Bill Hanson, who developed a water management strategy that considers the needs of both loons and people on reservoirs; and our other colleagues across the country working for loon conservation, such as Doug Smith of Yellowstone National Park, who is actively spearheading the recovery of Wyoming's population. Our friendship with many of these colleagues runs decades long, and speaks to the camaraderie shared from our unique privilege of working with loons.

We place value on the things we care for, and that compels us toward further study and action. Grassroots organizations dedicated to loon conservation have brought concerned citizens together with biologists to document and safeguard the natural cycles and places of loons. From these efforts, many states have seen their loon populations recover from lows in the 1970s to healthier numbers today—particularly in New England, New York, Wisconsin, Minnesota, and Montana. In Massachusetts, where populations were extirpated before 1900, breeding loons have been slowly returning since 1975. Even after decades of conservation efforts, breeding populations are still unstable in Idaho, Michigan, North Dakota, Washington, and Wyoming.

While state and federal wildlife agencies have fewer resources available in proportion to the conservation challenges ahead, private organizations and individuals are needed more than ever to compensate for that loss of critical revenue. One example of such collaboration is *Restore the Call*, a scientific initiative to restore and recover loon populations to their former range. The work of this project is made possible through a generous grant from the Ricketts Conservation Foundation, working in partnership with

Long-term conservation efforts in the Northeast and Great Lakes region have resulted in stronger populations. Moving forward, conservation efforts will continue in the East, but will also focus in the West on small, isolated, and declining loon populations such as in northwestern Wyoming.

loon biologists from Biodiversity Research Institute. This joint, national initiative provides an opportunity to strengthen current loon populations, bringing together wildlife biologists from governmental agencies, universities, and the private sector, and working across multiple state borders to address the major threats to loons at a population-level scale.

While we need to continue a compassionate discourse on what it means to know loons and work for their survival, the value of loons, however, is more profound than the science. For many of us, a starry night and a chorus of loons are both nourishment and respite. To care about loons is to fully know we are less without their companionship.

"I'VE ALWAYS LOVED THAT SEASON WHEN THE LAKE ICE GROWS DARK AND THE AIR FIRST SMELLS LIKE FISHING OR BASEBALL. KEEP LOOKING SKYWARD THEN, AND YOU MIGHT SEE A LOON SEEKING OUT THE FIRST OPEN WATER ON ITS NESTING LAKE. MORE THAN TRILLIUM OR TROUT LILY, THAT LOON OFFERS THE FIRST SURE SIGN OF A NORTH COUNTRY SPRING."

— JEFF FAIR
    AUTHOR AND FIELD BIOLOGIST

SPRING:
Sojourn of Renewal

As the late winter days stretch into March, Common Loons appear resplendent in their full breeding plumage. Gone are the gray feathers of winter, replaced now with the familiar black velvet plumes distinctly patterned in white. The lengthening days trigger loons to start moving from their wintering areas on marine waters toward their breeding lakes.

While some individuals arrive in the southern periphery of their breeding range as early as mid to late March (typical in Washington, the lower Great Lakes, and southern New England), the majority of loons will initiate migratory flights in early to mid April, continuing along either the Atlantic or Pacific coasts.

Once in flight, loons travel swiftly, averaging a steady 60–75 mph for up to 12 hours per day. They fly only during the day, using landscape cues to track direction.

A migrating loon is a solitary traveler. Individual loons make their pilgrimage northward independent of their mates (pair bonds persist only during the breeding season). En route, individuals may form groups when they land and encounter other loons, usually at staging areas or other common areas where large numbers rest and feed.

The slow thaw of ice and gradual appearance of open water on their fresh-water breeding lakes will ultimately determine the timing of the loons' arrival on their summer waters.

As loons finally reach their breeding lakes, experienced male loons arrive on territory first. These seasoned loons know this journey and these waters. They have already successfully held territories here and raised young. Their early arrival gives them an advantage; they now have the time to feed and regain energy reserves after the long, taxing migration and before the need to reclaim a mate and defend a territory. The arrival of established males can precede similarly experienced females by several days, followed later by those less experienced, including first-time breeders, sometimes four to six weeks later. For these younger adult loons, the challenge of competing with established loons will be a test of instinct, and will mark a season of learning.

While loons carry a strong reputation for returning to the same lake each year, scientific studies of banded loons have shown that this is not always true. On average, eight out of ten adult loons return to territories held in previous years. Some adults return to the same lake, but move to new coves after losing their territory to a rival. Others may relocate to a neighboring lake after losing such a contest. Rarely do adult loons venture to lakes more than two to three miles from their former territories.

For loons, fidelity lies with their territory, not with their mate; this attachment to a site by both male and female drives regular pairing of the same individuals from year to

year. It is rare for the same pair to remain together for more than seven years.

The primary goal of loon pairs during the spring season is to acquire and maintain a territory in optimal habitat for raising young. Ideal lake size varies. Some loons nest on lakes as small as 13 acres, but most loon pairs select waterbodies greater than 60 acres. When lakes exceed 200 acres in size, there may be enough room for two pairs. Much larger lakes may have 50 or more pairs of loons. Lakes and reservoirs with clear water and an abundance of small fish provide the best habitats because loons are visual predators primarily focused on fish. Other features such as irregular shoreline configurations, presence of isolated coves, and multiple nesting islands contribute to habitat quality.

In the first few days of arrival, loon pairs spend much of their time feeding and recuperating from their migratory flights. Arriving loons pay particular attention to feather maintenance and waterproofing through wing flapping and preening. Manic bouts of acrobatic bathing on the water's surface regularly ensue, serving to remove feather mites. As the nesting period draws closer, interactions and calling with other loons increase.

Territorial loons regularly face challengers—intruders searching for a breeding territory and testing territory holders. It is common to see loons chasing one another underwater and wing-rowing across lakes during these springtime duels. In the more intense battles, adult loons lock their bills together and hit one another with the forward joints of their wings. Though rare, some encounters may end in death.

The cycle of migration, recuperation, procurement of territories, selection of mates, and the challenges of interlopers serve as prelude to the demands of nesting and chick-rearing ahead.

The primary goal of loon pairs during the spring season is to acquire and maintain a territory in optimal habitat for raising young.

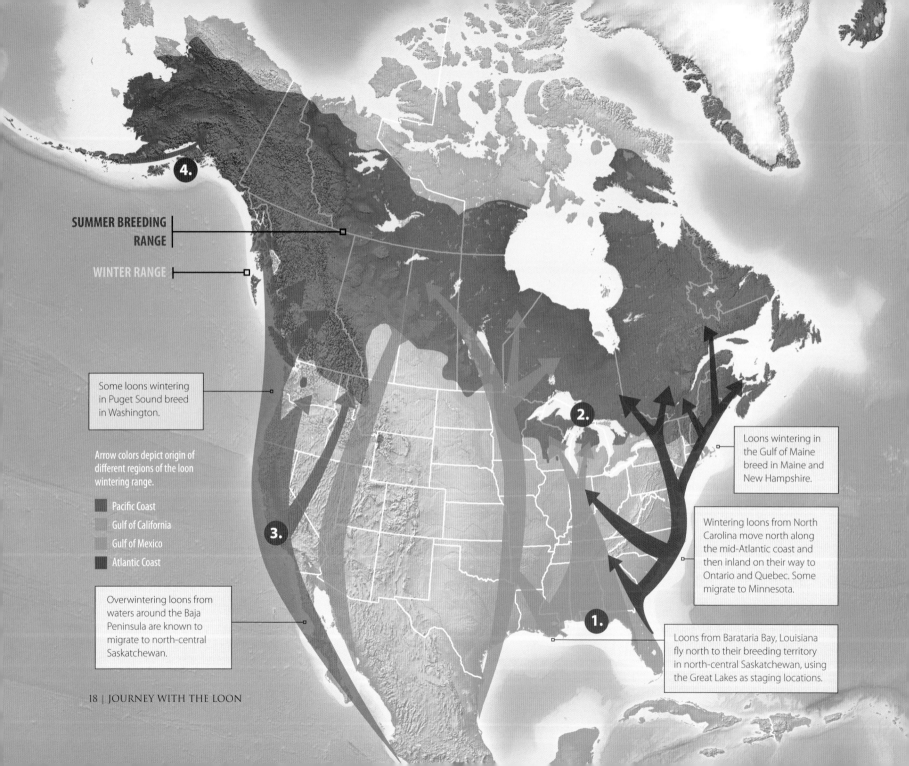

SUMMER BREEDING RANGE

WINTER RANGE

Some loons wintering in Puget Sound breed in Washington.

Arrow colors depict origin of different regions of the loon wintering range.

■ Pacific Coast
■ Gulf of California
■ Gulf of Mexico
■ Atlantic Coast

Overwintering loons from waters around the Baja Peninsula are known to migrate to north-central Saskatchewan.

Loons wintering in the Gulf of Maine breed in Maine and New Hampshire.

Wintering loons from North Carolina move north along the mid-Atlantic coast and then inland on their way to Ontario and Quebec. Some migrate to Minnesota.

Loons from Barataria Bay, Louisiana fly north to their breeding territory in north-central Saskatchewan, using the Great Lakes as staging locations.

SPRING VIEWING HOTSPOTS

1. **Apalachicola Bay, Florida.** This bay harbors thousands of loons from the Gulf of Mexico, readying for migration north to the Great Lakes and into central Canadian provinces. **Best viewing time: early April.**

2. **Whitefish Point, Michigan.** This is one of the best places to view groups of loons migrating above and at eye level. **Best viewing time: early May.**

3. **Goleta Point, Santa Barbara, California.** This is a good viewing point for Common Loons as well as tens of thousands of Pacific Loons. **Best viewing time: mid April.**

4. **Homer Spit, Alaska.** This bay hosts migrating Common Loons as well as Pacific Loons, Red-throated Loons, and sometimes Yellow-billed Loons. **Best viewing time: mid May.**

SPRING JOURNEYS OF THE COMMON LOON

We know the major migration routes and staging areas used by Common Loons through observations, recoveries of uniquely numbered leg bands, and satellite telemetry transmissions. The urge to return to freshwater breeding lakes of the northern United States and Canada starts in early March. An estimated 621,000 adult loons undertake the spring migration back to their breeding waters—around 435,000 (70 percent) from the Atlantic coast and 186,000 loons (30 percent) from the Pacific coast.

By early April, loons have either congregated in the Gulf of Mexico to make the leap northward to the Great Lakes, or are flying north along the coastlines. Loons migrate only during the day, initiating long-distance flights at dawn. Overland migration altitudes may range from 5,000 to nearly 9,000 feet, as measured by radar in New York. While migrating over water, loons fly typically 100-300 feet above the surface.

Loons with longer migration routes are typically smaller, while loons with shorter migrations tend to be larger. For example, loons from the interior part of North America, such as in Manitoba and Alberta where travel routes are more than 2,000 miles, average just over 7 pounds for females and 9 pounds for males. Conversely, in Maine, where loons may migrate a distance of just a few miles to nearly 100 miles, females average 10½ pounds, while males average 13 pounds and range up to 16½ pounds.

BIRD OBSERVATORIES PROVIDE VIEWING SITES

More than 35 bird observatories across North America have monitored migrating bird populations for decades. Most of these are located at prime migration points, where landscape features such as mountains, river valleys, and peninsulas funnel migrating birds. Using standardized methodologies that allow for long-term monitoring and geographic comparisons, observatories provide a quantitative basis for determining population trends and migratory paths.

In the Great Lakes Region, Whitefish Point Bird Observatory has been monitoring and documenting the annual migration of birds through a phenomenal concentration spot for migrant waterbirds since 1979. Whitefish Point is one of the best locations for watching large numbers of migrant Common Loons. From this site, researchers have been able to produce a long-term database on the magnitude and timing of the spring migration of loons. Here, peak migration for Common Loons generally falls within the first 10 days of May, and daily counts may exceed 1,000 loons.

*A migrating loon is often a solitary traveler, flying during the day,
using landscape cues to track direction.*

WHO HAS EVER PADDLED A
CANOE, OR CAST A FLY, OR
PITCHED A TENT IN THE NORTH
WOODS AND HAS NOT STOPPED
TO LISTEN TO THIS WAIL OF
THE WILDERNESS? AND WHAT
WOULD THE WILDERNESS BE
WITHOUT IT?"
    — A.C. BENT
        AUTHOR AND ORNITHOLOGIST

As part of the five- to six-minute preening bout, loons will shake their bodies in an upward pose.

A wing flap usually ends the preening bout. Wing flaps also help realign the feathers.

Loons are Faithful to Their Breeding Territory

On average, 80 percent of males and 82 percent of females return to their previous year's breeding territory. The ability of a loon to hold a territory and return in subsequent years depends heavily on the type of breeding territory it defends, which relates to the size of the lake and availability of prey.

Whole lake territories are typically smaller lakes (less than 200 acres) where one loon pair is able to protect the entire lake from trespass by another pair. Because they encounter fewer intrusions and disruptions by other loons, pairs on whole lake territories are generally more successful at fledging young than pairs from other territory types. *Multiple lake territories* occur on lakes small enough (less than 60 acres) that the breeding loons regularly fly off the nesting lake to feed on nearby lakes.

Partial lake territories result when loons breeding on larger lakes (more than 200 acres) compete for territories in coves, bays, and around islands. Larger lakes support more territories and also provide common foraging areas used by both breeding pairs and nonbreeding loons. Therefore, partial lake territories create more opportunity for single loons to test territory holders. For example, Moosehead Lake in Maine supports more than 50 loon territories across its 75,000 acres and on Lake Vermilion in Minnesota 55 territorial pairs are found on more than 40,000 acres of water.

The highest rate of annual territorial fidelity occurs on whole lake territories and is lowest for loons occupying multiple lake territories.

Loons migrating from the Gulf of Mexico may travel as far north as central Canada, even stopping in Chesapeake Bay before reaching their breeding lakes.

Territorial challenges peak shortly after arrival in the spring.

The defeated loon wing-rows away from the battle.

With territories defined, the pair now focuses on renewing their bond.

"THE CANOE WAS DRIFTING OFF THE ISLANDS,
AND THE TIME HAD COME FOR THE CALLING,
THAT MOMENT OF MAGIC IN THE NORTH
WHEN ALL IS QUIET AND THE WATER STILL
IRIDESCENT WITH THE FADING GLOW OF
SUNSET. EVEN THE SHORES SEEMED HUSHED
AND WAITING FOR THE FIRST LONE CALL.
WHEN IT CAME, A SINGLE LONG-DRAWN
MOURNFUL NOTE, THE QUIET WAS DEEPER
THAN BEFORE."

— SIGURD OLSON
AUTHOR AND NATURALIST

SUMMER:
Season of Place and Legacy

Summer defines the journey of the loon. Male and female loons, alike in their black and white plumage, have secured their territories and become reacquainted on their lakes. Against a backdrop of tall pine trees and deep, clear water, pairs choose their nest sites, secretly mate, engage in the vigil of incubation, and hatch and rear their young.

Courtship among loon pairs is quiet and subtle; a series of soft vocalizations between the pair and simultaneous bill dipping in close proximity of one another characterize the simple ritual.

During the courtship period, the male selects a site where both adults work together to build their nest. Loons prefer to nest on the shoreline edge of small islands or quiet coves, favoring sedge hummocks or floating bog mats. They construct their nests with whatever materials are readily available such as grass, moss, twigs, and mud. Some loons fashion elaborate nest bowls with piles of vegetation, while others assemble coarse stick structures. Depending on the territory, loons may simply lay their eggs in shallow scrapes in sand or even on hard rock.

When the nest is ready, the female lays one to two eggs, each about five inches long, olive colored, and speckled for camouflage. The loon pair shares the rigors of a month-long incubation period; during the day, the partners exchange sitting duties every four to six hours. There is little respite for either adult; when not on the nest, they feed, preen, and guard their territory against other loons. Females tend to sit for longer periods in the early days of incubation, especially at night when the males are often patrolling on the water, their distinctive yodels punctuating the night sky to warn other loons away.

Loons, not unlike other birds, are most sensitive to disturbance during the early part of incubation—even a thunderstorm can threaten a newly established clutch. As more time is invested, the adults become increasingly less likely to abandon the nest. Throughout incubation, nesting loons turn their eggs to ensure the contents will not adhere to the sides of the shell. They rarely leave their eggs uncovered, as this would make them vulnerable to overexposure to cold, heat, or predation. An unprotected egg is easy prey for gulls, ravens, crows, mink, and raccoons. Overall, incubating adults attend to their eggs more than 95 percent of the time.

Loons connect more to their territory than to each other. A failed nest signals a window of opportunity for a nonbreeding loon to intrude on the territory. During an intrusion, males attempt to displace other males, and females attempt to force out their counterparts. Confrontations between the pair and an intruding adult can result in a *circle dance*, a synchronized exhibition by the territorial pair to demonstrate their fitness. Watching the display, the nonterritorial

loon assesses its chances of taking over the territory. Based on the result of this contest, the lone loon can usurp both a territory and the mate. If an intrusion is not successful and the pair bond holds, the pair may renest within the next two weeks. If a second nesting attempt is not made, the pair simply maintains its presence on the lake for the summer. The ability to maintain a territory will bode well for retaining that territory in subsequent years.

At the end of incubation, chicks emerge from the shell within a day of each other (known as an *asynchronous hatch*). Sequential hatching gives the first chick a head start at successfully attracting parental attention and securing food.

Newly hatched chicks are buoyant during their first few days and have difficulty maneuvering. Protection by the adults is essential for survival, and therefore loon families stay close, softly hooting to one another to maintain contact. In these early days, loon chicks seek rest and refuge from cold water and predators by riding on the backs of the adults.

Adults catch small fish and insects, such as dragonfly larvae, and transfer prey from their bill tip to the chick. Until chicks molt completely out of their downy feathers, they tire easily and are susceptible to predators such as pike, bass, snapping turtles, and Bald Eagles. After six weeks of age, chicks display more advanced skills, including capturing prey underwater. By summer's end, they can feed and fend for themselves, and have begun the first steps toward full flight.

Summer represents a major progression in the loon's journey. Chicks of this year will return to their natal lakes as breeding adults in three years time. A season rich in learning and growing, it is during the summer when loons establish the cycle of place and legacy.

Against a backdrop
of tall pine trees
and deep, clear water,
pairs choose their
nest sites, secretly mate,
engage in the vigil
of incubation,
and hatch and rear
their young.

In western and central northern Canada, the breeding range edge for Common Loons follows the edge of the taiga zone.

Unlike in other parts of its range, the Common Loon breeds in tundra habitats of Iceland, Greenland, northern Quebec, and southern Baffin Island and west of Hudson Bay in Nunavut.

SUMMER BREEDING RANGE

In north-central Saskatchewan, breeding loons tracked through satellite transmitters show that lakes may contain individuals that overwinter from both the Atlantic and Pacific coasts.

The thousands of pothole lakes found in the prairies are not suitable for nesting loons as they lack the fish biomass needed by a loon family (nearly 1,000 pounds needed).

SUMMER RANGE FOR YOUNG LOONS (1- AND 2-YEAR-OLDS)

Young oversummering loons are often found along the North Carolina coastline.

5.

3.

2.

1.

4.

SUMMER VIEWING HOTSPOTS

1. **Acadia National Park, Maine.** Loon breeding territories are found on most of the interior lakes and nonbreeding loons are present along the coastline.

2. **Adirondack Mountains, New York.** A robust and growing population of breeding loons is monitored by Biodiversity Research Institute's Adirondack Center for Loon Conservation program.

3. **Voyageurs National Park, Minnesota.** Breeding loons can be easily and frequently viewed in close quarters by kayak, canoe, or houseboat.

4. **Yellowstone National Park, Wyoming.** Only 14 breeding pairs remain in Wyoming and more than half of those pairs are in the Park (viewing spots may be accessible only by long hikes).

5. **Kenai National Wildlife Refuge, Alaska.** A canoe trail within the Refuge provides great viewing of breeding Common Loons.

Best viewing time for all locations: June–August.

SUMMER JOURNEYS OF THE COMMON LOON

The Common Loon's breeding range is restricted to freshwater habitats of North America (including Greenland) and Iceland. In Canada and Alaska, loons are generally found nesting north to the edge of the taiga shield. There are exceptions, however. Common Loons nest on the tundra and coastal plains of Baffin Island and west of Hudson Bay in Nunavut, the Ungava Peninsula in Quebec, Greenland, and Iceland. In central and western North America, these types of open habitats are instead occupied by the Yellow-billed Loon.

According to historical accounts, the southern extent of the Common Loon's breeding range has retracted. Nesting records from states without an existing breeding population include California, Illinois, Indiana, Iowa, Ohio, Oregon, and Pennsylvania. After impressive conservation actions by governmental agencies and nonprofit organizations, a reversal of breeding range retractions began in the 1970s and continues today for much of the United States. Most notable breeding range improvements have been found in the New England states and in New York, but progress can also be found in Minnesota, Montana, and Wisconsin. Breeding populations are still unstable, or declining, in Idaho, Michigan, North Dakota, Washington, and Wyoming.

In summer, nonbreeding loons may also be found throughout much of the United States south of the breeding range—on both lakes and the ocean. Not all adult loons are on a breeding territory. For 20 percent of the adult population (or more), nonbreeding individuals wander extensively and are commonly found on both freshwater and saltwater systems. Meanwhile, for two and one-half years, subadult loons remain primarily on the ocean, generally moving northward along the coast during the summer and southward during the winter.

Male loons choose the nest site; both share in nest construction.

Male and female loons share equally in the duties
of incubation.

"THAT NIGHT IT WAS STILL, AND IN THE MOONLIGHT THE LOONS BEGAN AS I HAD HEARD THEM BEFORE, FIRST THE WILD, EXCITED CALLING OF A GROUP OF BIRDS DASHING ACROSS THE WATER, THEN ANSWERS FROM THE OTHER GROUPS UNTIL THE ENTIRE EXPANSE OF THE LAKE WAS FULL OF THEIR MUSIC. WE SAT AROUND UNTIL LONG AFTER DARK AND LISTENED."

— SIGURD OLSON
AUTHOR AND NATURALIST

THE LANGUAGE OF LOONS

Loon language is comprised of four basic calls: the tremolo, yodel, wail, and hoot. The *tremolo*, commonly referred to as the "laugh" of the loon, is more aptly described as an indicator of stress or anxiety. Voiced rapidly, the tremolo increases in intensity and frequency dependent on the level of the perceived threat. The tremolo, the only call made in flight, is also used to determine if other loons are occupying a lake below.

The *yodel*, voiced only by males, is a territorial song. Until recently, evidence indicated yodels were unique signatures of individuals. Through observations of banded males, we now know that yodels may be a signature of a territory; male loons may alter or mimic yodels when changing territories.

The *wail* is a long-distance contact call—a way to communicate to other loon "neighbors" on the same or nearby lakes. Wails also help mates locate each other. The *hoot*, a softer, quieter call than the others, is used for short-range calls among family members.

Loons will use several variations of these four calls to communicate more complex expressions. On larger lakes, multiple loon pairs will regularly communicate with one another through night chorusing. While this allows for individuals to "check" on the status of other loons in their neighborhood during the night hours, it is a memorable reverie for those lucky enough to hear it.

Incubation lasts 27 to 30 days.

Eggs are rarely left unattended. The adults turn the eggs often to prevent the contents from adhering to the inside of the shell.

"THE PRESENT WAS AN EGG LAID BY THE PAST
THAT HAD THE FUTURE INSIDE ITS SHELL."
— ZORA NEALE HURSTON
AUTHOR AND ANTHROPOLOGIST

Loons generally lay two eggs, olive colored and speckled
for camouflage.

Loons vigorously defend their territory;
the adult at left chases a female Hooded Merganser.
The "penguin dance" (above) is a typical
defensive posture.

After hatch, loon chicks almost immediately leave the nest.

Young chicks back ride for warmth, rest, and protection.

A chick commonly rides on the back of its parent,
and sometimes both manage to fit.

"I ALWAYS WANT TO FREEZE TIME WHEN SUMMER ARRIVES IN NEW ENGLAND, AND LOON PAIRS ON MY FAVORITE PONDS BEGIN TO HATCH CHICKS. NOTHING HIGHLIGHTS NATURE'S CANVAS WITH MORE ALLURE, OR CAPTIVATES ME MORE FULLY.

I WISH FOR LONGER DAYS AND CALM WATERS, GOOD LOON PARENTS, AND IGNORANT PREDATORS. I WISH THAT EVERY CHICK SURVIVES LONG ENOUGH FOR AT LEAST ONE BACK RIDE. THAT'S A MAGIC MOMENT, BRIEF, FOR ALL TO WITNESS, AND FOR PHOTOGRAPHERS TO CAPTURE AND PRETEND TO STOP TIME."

— LEE ATTIX
Loon Field Biologist

"LIVE IN THE SUNSHINE, SWIM THE SEA,
DRINK THE WILD AIR."

— RALPH WALDO EMERSON
POET AND ESSAYIST

At about five weeks of age, contour feathers
start to replace downy feathers.

LOON CHICK DEVELOPMENT — FIRST MONTH

Week 1: Newly-hatched chicks have brownish-black down. Buoyancy and lack of maneuverability leave them vulnerable to predators above and below the water. Development is rapid during this week.

Week 2: Chicks are now seven times their hatching weight and their down covering begins to appear more brown than black. Chicks at this age are capable of shallow dives for short periods. Back riding during the first two weeks is common.

Week 3: A chick's foot development is rapid and disproportionate to the rest of its body. Large webbed feet are needed for swimming, aiding in food capture, and evading predators. Chicks this age, now almost half the length of the adults, back ride less frequently.

Week 4: At one month, loon chicks remain fully down-covered but appear more unkempt. The bill is noticeably longer at this stage in development.

Week 5: The first gray contour feathers begin to replace downy feathers on the upper back. Flight feathers appear along the leading edge of the wing. The initial growth of the flight feathers is evident in this photo.

Week 6: Gray contour feathers are now apparent on the back, as well as the wing. At this age, chicks are greater than half the length of the adults. Six-week-old chicks have a streamlined appearance that allows for greater ability to catch fish and escape predators.

Week 7: By seven weeks, chicks have more gray contour feathers than brown down. At this age until they fledge, mortality is relatively low. Feeding, however, continues to be supplemented by the adults.

Week 8: Only small tufts of brown down may still be evident on the head, neck, and tail region. If food is not a limiting factor, two chicks can survive and fledge from a lake.

Loon Chick Development — Third Month

Week 9: At this age, loon chicks are fully covered in smooth contour feathers.

Week 10: Flight feathers are now completely in and chicks will be engaged in more wing flapping and stretching behaviors.

Week 11: During their eleventh week, chicks are practicing takeoffs in preparation of learning full flight. Chicks will model the techniques of the adults through numerous test runs.

Week 12: Chicks are fully capable of flight at this age, but usually remain on their natal lake for a few more weeks. Twelve-week-old chicks are able to fend for themselves and have nearly reached full adult size.

Loon Chick Development — Subadults

Week 13: Chicks are now fully capable of sustained flight and may fly to neighboring lakes.

Week 14: Loon chicks are independent. The adults will leave them to migrate back to their wintering areas.

Young loons can fend for themselves by ten weeks of age,
however they still seek parental care.

"WE MISS THE EYES OF BIRDS,
FOCUSING ONLY ON FEATHERS."
— TERRY TEMPEST WILLIAMS
   AUTHOR AND ENVIRONMENTALIST

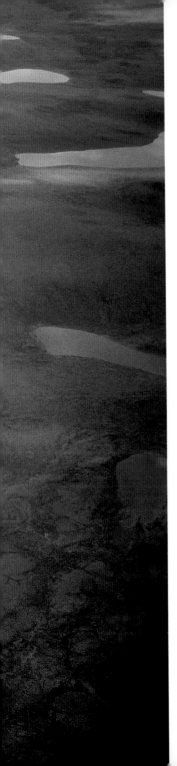

Small populations of Common Loons breed in the treeless coastal plains and tundra regions, such as in Greenland.

To Band a Loon

Marking birds with unique leg bands is one of the most long-standing methods of studying birds. Loons are important indicators of water quality and overall health of aquatic environments, and as such have long been a high profile species. However, due to their agility in the water, they are elusive.

Since 1989, when we discovered a reliable and replicable method for capturing loons, researchers began to band individual loons, which presented opportunities to conduct demographic, behavioral, and contaminant studies. From data gathered, we now understand the importance of certain individuals in the population—generally, half of the chicks produced each year originate from only 20 percent of the total breeding population.

Through observing banded loons, we now have a better understanding of the connectivity between breeding and wintering locations. For example, in winter, loons from Maine simply move to the Maine coast, loons in Wisconsin migrate to Florida, and Montana loons overwinter on the coast of California. While the loon's lifespan remains relatively undefined, to date, the oldest living banded loon is 27 years old and counting.

Wildlife biologists and collaborators at Biodiversity Research Institute have now caught and banded more than 5,000 loons. The capture of loons is not taken lightly; each individual loon is treated with great care and respect and each will contribute to a large dataset of information detailing the intricacies of loon natural history.

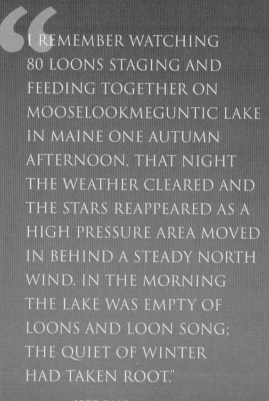

"I REMEMBER WATCHING
80 LOONS STAGING AND
FEEDING TOGETHER ON
MOOSELOOKMEGUNTIC LAKE
IN MAINE ONE AUTUMN
AFTERNOON. THAT NIGHT
THE WEATHER CLEARED AND
THE STARS REAPPEARED AS A
HIGH PRESSURE AREA MOVED
IN BEHIND A STEADY NORTH
WIND. IN THE MORNING
THE LAKE WAS EMPTY OF
LOONS AND LOON SONG;
THE QUIET OF WINTER
HAD TAKEN ROOT."

— JEFF FAIR
   AUTHOR AND FIELD BIOLOGIST

FALL:
Rite of Passage

A subtle shift in light exposes the first turn of color on leaf tips and heralds in autumn, a time for unwinding the strict rhythms of summer. Although still under the care of the adults, young loons have been learning necessary life skills since summer's hatch, anticipating their first journey at the end of the season.

By early fall, chicks are cloaked in smooth gray feathers instead of the downy brown of new chicks. The contoured feathering of young loons is more streamlined, further enhancing their ability to dive and catch fish.

Like their chicks, adult loons change appearance in the fall. The lustrous black and white feathering of the summer loon, also known as the breeding or *alternate* plumage, is replaced by the gray-brown of winter, or *basic* plumage. The timing of this process, referred to as molting, is likely dependent on changing hormones, individual age, and even environmental stressors. Growing new feathers requires an energetic investment, and therefore molting coincides with periods of less strenuous demands, such as when chicks become more independent.

The first signs of molting appear as a silver-gray shadow at the base of a loon's bill, and then progresses across the head and over the upper back. Flight feathers remain unaffected during this fall transition since they are necessary for the migration ahead.

Loon pairs are territorial through the summer. As the leaves turn, chicks become more self-reliant, allowing the adults to relax their vigilance. They leave their young for periods of time to socialize with other adults on their lake or nearby lakes.

Researchers are working to fully understand the benefit of these social gatherings. We do know that these groups include loons that have reared chicks in that season, those that held their territories even if they did not produce chicks, and nonterritorial loons (those without partners and without claim to a territory). Evidence suggests that messages are conveyed among adults about the reproductive success occurring within the neighborhood. This type of information is important for loons that have not secured territories, setting the stage for them to identify prime territories for the following year.

While researchers look more closely at fall migration patterns, we know one adult leaves the family first, usually followed by the second adult within a few weeks. The chicks are left to migrate by themselves. Some adult loons, especially those without young, leave their breeding lakes in late summer, but most begin their journey south in the latter part of September or October.

In fall, as in spring, loons set out individually in migration, but they stage (gather to rest and feed together) in groups of hundreds and even thousands as they move toward wintering areas. Loons

reaching their destinations along the mid-Atlantic coast in November time their arrival with the movements of their favored prey species, the Atlantic menhaden, a herring that swims in large schools near the surface at this time of year.

Unlike most other birds, Common Loons vary widely in body size; a male in Maine might weigh twice as much as a male in interior Canada. Body size correlates to the distance loons must fly from wintering to breeding locations—the farther the distance, the smaller their body size. For example, loons that breed in Saskatchewan, Canada travel more than 2,000 miles to reach winter destinations on the Atlantic or Pacific coasts. Female loons from this area of central Canada average just over 7 pounds and males average just over 8½ pounds.

Conversely, loons that breed close to their wintering ocean waters, such as those in Alaska and Maine, travel shorter distances during migration and are therefore larger in size. Male loons from Alaska average over 12½ pounds and those from Maine average more than 13 pounds.

Back on the breeding lakes, the chicks linger, sometimes into November if the water remains free of ice. Persistent practice flights develop gradually into smoother takeoffs and touch downs, allowing these young loons to depart the natal lake with confidence. Once they leave, chicks are now termed *juveniles* and retain that status until they reach one year of age.

Late autumn brings a sharpening chill across the water's surface, freezing the shallow edges. The ice ultimately compels the last of the loons to leave these waters before the long silence of winter descends.

Although still under the care of the adults, young loons have been learning necessary life skills since summer's hatch, anticipating their first journey at the end of the season.

Loons from Iceland and likely eastern Greenland migrate southeast to Western Europe.

Lake Ontario is an important staging area on the Great Lakes for loons originating from Ontario and Quebec, which represent the largest breeding population of loons.

Breeding loons from the Kenai Peninsula in Alaska have a short migration to their wintering waters around Kodiak Island.

Arrow colors depict ultimate wintering destinations by general regions.

- Pacific Coast
- Gulf of California
- Gulf of Mexico
- Atlantic Coast

Large numbers of loons stage on reservoirs created by the Tennessee Valley Authority in Tennessee and surrounding states.

Thousands of loons arrive in Chesapeake Bay in mid November, timed with large numbers of menhaden. Some loons remain here for the winter, others move further south in December into coastal North Carolina.

This is the location of the Cape May Bird Observatory and their seabird monitoring program Avalon Sea Watch. Fall counts of more than 5,000 Common Loons were typical in the 1990s; for unknown reasons, recent counts are lower, only numbering 1,000 and 2,000 loons. **Best viewing time: late October to mid November.**

2. Finger Lakes, New York. Upwards of 3,500 migrating loons pass through Taughannock Falls at the southern end of Cayuga Lake. **Best viewing time: mid to late November.**

3. Lake Winnibigoshish and Mille Lacs, Minnesota. More than 1,000 loons can often be observed flocking together. **Best viewing time: mid to late October.**

4. Walker Lake, Nevada. Walker Lake and nearby Pyramid Lake are important staging areas for central Canadian breeding populations. While daily counts of nearly 1,400 loons occurred in the 1990s, documented changes in habitat quality have substantially decreased the number of loons currently using Walker Lake. **Best viewing time: mid October.**

5. Point Reyes National Seashore, California. This is the location of Point Blue, a bird-oriented conservation and research group. While standardized fall migration counts of loons at Point Reyes have not been conducted, it is an accessible and well-known observation place for migrant loons. **Best viewing time: October and November.**

FALL JOURNEYS OF THE COMMON LOON

The southerly movement of fall migrants represents more than 725,000 loons, including approximately 105,000 young-of-the-year (those loons hatched in a particular summer).

Adult loons begin to leave their freshwater breeding territories in September or October, and arrive at their wintering destinations as late as December. Fall migration follows a more leisurely pace than the spring journey; there is no pressure in fall for the loons to establish breeding territories, so the loons can stop more often.

En route, large numbers of loons congregate (or stage) on large lakes to rest and feed. Staging groups can sometimes number in the thousands. Sizeable lakes found midway between breeding lakes and wintering areas, such as Lake Winnibigoshish and Mille Lacs in Minnesota, Flathead Lake in Montana, and Walker Lake in Nevada, are well known staging areas for loons.

Loon populations from Ontario and Quebec (on the order of 350,000 adults) primarily stage on Lake Erie and Lake Ontario. Thousands of these migrants cross over New York's Finger Lakes arriving in Chesapeake Bay in early November. Other staging areas include the large reservoirs across the interior of the United States.

On these stopover lakes and reservoirs, loons forage individually or in small groups. In the evenings, loons gather to form larger groups, sometimes numbering more than 1,000 individuals in a single flock.

"EVERY NATURAL ACTION IS GRACEFUL."

— RALPH WALDO EMERSON
Poet and Essayist

ADAPTED TO AQUATIC LIFE

Aquatic birds, loons are structurally designed for life in the water. In summer, they breed on freshwater lakes; in winter, they generally live within nearshore areas of the ocean. Loons are heavy bodied, with dense bones and large feet adapted for exceptional underwater abilities such as swimming, diving, and maneuvering quickly to capture prey.

Europeans refer to the Common Loon as the Great Northern Diver because these birds can dive with submarine-like capabilities, quietly sinking below the water's surface without a ripple to escape detection. Loons can remain underwater for three minutes or longer, but usually they time their dives to last for less than one minute.

When submerged, loons control their buoyancy by compressing air sacs in their abdomen and squeezing their feathers tightly to force out any trapped air. Compared to their body size, their narrow wings have a relatively small surface area; broad wings would keep a loon too buoyant to dive deeply or quickly enough to catch fish, their main prey.

Unlike the hollow bones of most birds, the bones of loons are more solid than hollow, which further aids in their diving capabilities. Although loons usually dive in shallower water, they do have the ability to reach depths greater than 180 feet.

The fall molt begins at the bill and includes only body feathers;
flight feathers are needed for the journey to wintering locations.
In the fall, it is common to find young loons remaining
together, lingering longer before they, too, depart.

Loon pairs are territorial through the summer,
but as the leaves turn, chicks become more self-reliant,
allowing the adults to relax their vigilance.

"IN THE FALL THE LOON CAME, AS USUAL,
TO MOULT AND BATHE IN THE POND,
MAKING THE WOODS RING WITH HIS
WILD LAUGHTER."
— HENRY DAVID THOREAU
Poet and Naturalist

*In fall, adult loons may be seen in small or even large
groups, socializing before migration.*

LOONS IN FLIGHT

When in the water, loons maneuver with great skill and agility. The tradeoff is that they must work harder in flight.

Loons require a long "runway" to gain lift; while actively flapping their wings, they run on the water's surface, sometimes up to several hundred feet before takeoff. Once in the air, they are strong fliers, averaging speeds up to 75 mph and sometimes traveling more than 2,000 miles during a migration stint.

The ratio of a bird's weight to the size of its wings (including wing length and surface area) is a critical component of flight performance. This relationship is referred to as wing loading. The greater a bird's wing load, the faster it must fly to stay airborne. Loons must flap their wings about 260 times per minute to stay aloft, unable to rely on gliding or soaring like other birds. High wing loading also decreases a bird's maneuverability in flight. Loon wings have a small surface area relative to body weight, which is an advantage underwater, but this body type requires more energy during flight. Among all North American birds, loons demonstrate one of the highest wing loading values—they are designed best for life in the water, not in the sky.

Loons may travel long distances during migration;
along the way they utilize different habitats
such as desert lakes to stop and rest.

Loons leave these waters before
the long silence of winter descends.

WINTER:
RETURN TO THE SEA

As ice creeps across the surface of lakes on the breeding grounds, the coastal wintering waters welcome the adults, as well as a new generation of loons. Common Loons spend as much of their lives at sea as they do on their breeding lakes. This split lifestyle requires an ability to manage the physiological and environmental challenges associated with transitioning from freshwater to marine habitats.

Once loons are ocean-bound, they consume the majority of their fresh water from the bodies of swallowed prey. In addition, they are able to extract the salt from ingested seawater by using a hormonally controlled salt gland that is used when the loon first returns to the ocean. This gland concentrates salt into a solution that the loon excretes through external nares, or nostrils, in the upper bill. Loons effectively "sneeze" out surplus salt.

Wintering loons are found mostly along nearshore coastal waters including channels, coves, and bays; they also utilize inland waters, which provide protection from storms. Loons can also be found many miles offshore, anywhere they can access fish in the water column or on the bottom, but they are rarely found beyond the continental shelf.

Based on wintering loon studies in Morro Bay, California, adult loons return to the same areas each winter and appear to frequent loosely defined feeding areas. Overall, the use of specific marine habitats by loons is dictated by the availability of prey, which is influenced by water clarity, depth, salinity gradients, and tidal changes.

The daily activities of wintering loons center on feeding. Loons find their prey primarily by sight, employing one of two foraging strategies: 1) solitary feeding where prey items are more dispersed and near

shore; and (2) flock feeding when schools of small fish, such as Atlantic menhaden and Gulf silversides, are present. The formation of feeding groups may also help to reduce risk from large predatory fish, such as sharks.

Winter storms and associated wave action increase seawater turbidity, which affects a loon's ability to see clearly when foraging for fish. During severe weather events that reduce visibility, loons switch from catching fish to hunting for crabs and other crustaceans. Loons may use their bills to locate these bottom dwellers, potentially probing their bills into the seabed. Although easier to capture than fish, crustaceans are not ideal prey because they provide fewer nutrients than fish.

With no need to protect nesting territories, loons are more tolerant of other birds during the winter months and will mingle with other species such as Common Eiders, Long-tailed Ducks, and Horned

Grebes. Loons continue to vocalize in winter, although less frequently than during the summer months. Hoots and short wails are most commonly heard when loons are in close contact with each other, such as in feeding flocks or when rafting together at night. Winter calls may also include the tremolo (a sign of stress), but territorial yodel calls are rarely heard.

Unlike ducks and geese, which undergo a wing molt prior to migration, loons "delay" their wing molt until they reach their wintering area. Rather than replacing their feathers gradually like other seabirds, they lose all their flight feathers simultaneously. During a three-week period occurring sometime during January through March, loons are flightless.

Maintaining and waterproofing the new growth of feathers becomes a vigilant duty, especially as the winter molt continues. Feather regeneration requires a great deal of body energy; during this time, loons are especially vulnerable to additional environmental stressors such as oil spills and severe weather patterns.

By winter's end, adult loons reclaim their striking breeding plumage and their energy reserves are ready for the journey back to their traditional freshwater breeding lakes.

The cycles of pilgrimage, triggered by instinct, refined with experience, and shaped in accordance with nature, constitute just a part of a loon's inheritance. Coded deep within every loon's essence lies the living paradigm for all seasons and successes of the loon's life journey.

Conservation of these creatures requires careful and considerate documentation of all parts of this wild heritage—not simply as a scientific inquiry, but as a human responsibility and a privilege.

Common Loons spend as much of their lives at sea as they do on their breeding lakes.

Nearly 5,000 loons overwinter in Europe, including Iceland.

WINTER RANGE

Puget Sound, Washington is home to the highest densities of wintering loons on the Pacific coast.

North Carolina harbors the highest density of known wintering loons.

Loons commonly overwinter in the Gulf of California. The desert landscape of the Baja California peninsula is a stark contrast to the North Woods habitat more typically associated with loons.

Barataria Bay, Louisiana is an overwintering location for loons breeding in north-central Saskatchewan.

WINTER VIEWING HOTSPOTS

1. **Ferry Beach Park in Scarborough, Maine.** Beach access provides accessible observation points for loons, especially those gathering at the mouth of the Scarborough River.

2. **Huntington Beach State Park near Myrtle Beach, South Carolina.** Loons are regularly viewed foraging just beyond the wave breaks and in small flocks during evening hours.

3. **Cedar Key, Florida.** Wintering loons are widely distributed across the relatively shallow waters of the Gulf of Mexico and can be viewed from the Cedar Key peninsula.

4. **Booker T. Washington State Park near Chattanooga, Tennessee.** Reservoirs created by the Tennessee Valley Authority, such as Chickamauga Lake, now support several thousand wintering loons.

5. **Morro Bay, California.** A large population of loons that have been studied and banded can be viewed here. Some of these loons are known to breed in Montana.

Best viewing time for all locations: December–March

WINTER JOURNEYS OF THE COMMON LOON

The winter range of the Common Loon covers an extensive, mostly coastal, area of North America.

Along the shores of the Pacific Ocean, loons range from the icy northern waters of the Alaskan Aleutian Islands, south across the kelp beds of California, to the cactus-lined shores of Mexico. Densities of loons on the Pacific coast are greatest around southern British Columbia and Puget Sound into Washington, southern California, and the northern part of the Gulf of California.

In the Gulf of Mexico, loons are most commonly found on the eastern shores where relatively shallow waters encourage broad, offshore use. West of the Florida panhandle, loon densities decline, with only a few individuals wintering south of the Texas-Mexico border.

On the Atlantic coast, loons rarely use the subtropical waters of the southernmost Florida peninsula, but they do overwinter north of this point, all the way to the cold rocky shores of Newfoundland. The highest densities of wintering loons on the East Coast are found in coastal waters off of North Carolina; loons are distributed offshore in lower densities to the edge of the continental shelf.

Loons are also found inland in some areas of the United States for part or all of the winter months. In particular, large reservoirs in eastern Tennessee and surrounding states are often used as wintering areas for an increasing number of loons. Even large and slow moving rivers, such as the Columbia River in Washington, are used by overwintering loons—sometimes in the thousands. The Great Lakes are not well used by loons in the winter, despite the perceived capacity of these lakes to support loons over the winter.

Data from marine surveys indicate that loons do not overwinter around Greenland, however, they do overwinter in Iceland. Several thousand loons winter in waters off the United Kingdom, with incidental records of loons occurring south to Portugal and east to Norway and Denmark.

Loons from north-central Canada overwinter in the
Gulf of California, along the shores of the
Baja California peninsula.

"NATURE IS NOT A PLACE TO VISIT.
IT IS HOME."
— GARY SNYDER
Poet and Environmentalist

Young Loons on the Ocean

Instinct guides a loon on its first journey to the ocean. Following pathways delineated by biology and landscape, juvenile loons reach their wintering grounds and many remain there for the next two and a half years. While adult loons return to familiar wintering areas, juveniles move more freely across broad coastal areas without any parental direction except what they inherited genetically. Here they must learn how to find new food sources and cope with the intensity of winter's weather.

In spring, while adults migrate once again to their freshwater breeding lakes, last summer's young, now nearly one year old, remain on coastal waters, flying north along the shorelines of the Atlantic or Pacific Oceans.

By June, the young gray-plumaged loons, now considered *subadults*, undergo their first complete wing-feather molt. Since the molt is energetically taxing and impedes proper waterproofing of new feathers, these loons often beach themselves to rest and dry out.

Shorter days and autumnal cold fronts trigger the young loons to travel to more southerly waters for their second winter. This pattern of moving up and down the coast is subsequently repeated for another summer-winter cycle. During these first two years, some subadults will fly to and spend time on inland freshwater lakes, although such sightings are relatively uncommon.

In the summer of their second year, loons molt into their breeding plumage for the first time. At three years of age, they embark on their journey back to the lakes in the area where they hatched. On average, these three-year-olds return to within 15 miles of their natal lake. Their inaugural migration, however, is delayed as they await the completion of their molt. Older adults molt in their flight feathers months earlier, and therefore leave in advance of the inexperienced loons.

When they do return to the breeding waters, young adults must compete with other loons, including established adults, to gain territories. It usually takes several seasons to learn the skills needed to locate and secure territories. On average, loons first attempt breeding at six years of age.

Loons transition from freshwater to marine environments during the winter months. When wave action reduces visibility, loons switch from fish to crustaceans for prey.

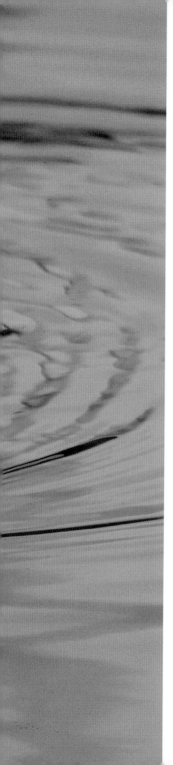

After arrival to the wintering grounds, loons molt their flight feathers; they are unable to fly for about a three-week period during this process.

Coded deep within every loon's essence
lies the living paradigm for all seasons and
success of the loon's life journey.

"THE NATION BEHAVES WELL IF IT TREATS THE NATURAL RESOURCES AS ASSETS, WHICH IT MUST TURN OVER TO THE NEXT GENERATION INCREASED, AND NOT IMPAIRED IN VALUE."
— THEODORE ROOSEVELT
President and Conservationist

Continuing the
Journey

" HOLD UP A MIRROR AND ASK YOURSELF WHAT YOU ARE
CAPABLE OF DOING, AND WHAT YOU REALLY CARE ABOUT.
THEN TAKE THE INITIATIVE—DON'T WAIT FOR SOMEONE
ELSE TO ASK YOU TO ACT."

— SYLVIA EARLE
Oceanographer and National Geographic's
Explorer-in-Residence

Making a Difference

*J**ourney with the Loon* encompasses the natural and essential cycles that comprise a loon's life. The knowledge shared within this book represents years of dedicated research conducted by wildlife biologists, photographers, and private individuals.

On these pages we have followed the Common Loon through migration, territorial conquest, mating, nesting, chick development, and final fledging. Chronicling the natural requirements and intimacies of every stage in the loon's life cycle is crucial for conservation and to ensure the continuing journey of the Common Loon. Securing a place for loons as a valued wildlife species is just part of our shared natural heritage—it is a responsibility entrusted to us from future generations.

What you can do

Become a member. There are numerous organizations across the country dedicated to loon conservation, and membership is critical to their missions. Consider volunteering, including participating in loon censuses, monitoring nest sites, and collecting reproductive data.

Become a steward. Participate with local lake associations to encourage responsible fishing practices, such as the use of non-lead tackle, low-impact shoreline development and responsible recreational activities. Create an awareness and appreciation for water quality, lake wildlife, and wetland areas that serve as nesting habitat.

Get involved. Larger issues, such as mercury contamination, require regulations that reduce use and emissions. Support legislation that improves efforts by local, state, and federal entities to better regulate pollution.

Leave a legacy. As resources from state and federal agencies become more limited and politicized, private donors are increasingly more vital in providing funding for environmental work. Consider contributing to efforts that preserve the integrity of wildlife and wild places.

MAKING A DIFFERENCE: GRASSROOTS CONSERVATION

The Loon Preservation Committee (LPC) was created in 1975 in response to dramatically declining loon populations in New Hampshire and concerns about the effects of human activities on loons. LPC works to preserve loons and their habitats through monitoring, research, management, and public education, all fostered by an extensive grassroots network of dedicated members and volunteers. Many of LPC's initiatives involve close coordination with federal and state agencies and other nonprofit organizations. LPC was one of the first organizations to show that coordinated and thoughtful human actions could reverse the decline of a threatened or endangered species. Our success has inspired the creation of state-wide, regional and even international organizations to preserve loons, and our efforts continue to benefit other species that depend on clean water, natural shorelines, and functioning ecosystems.

There is room left for loon populations to grow in New Hampshire, and work left for us to do. Despite our efforts and our progress, the Common Loon remains a threatened species in New Hampshire and faces growing challenges. The world has shrunk in the past four decades—today we are aware of the smallness of our planet and the interconnectedness of all things. New perils like global climate change are providing compelling evidence of our impacts on our world, with uncertain consequences for humans and wildlife. Through the years we have shown that loons can thrive in the company of people if we value them and respect their needs, and we will continue to work for informed choices and for wise stewardship of loons. If we've learned anything in our 40 years of work, it is that a caring and involved public is the key to preserving loons, or any wildlife species.

— Harry Vogel
   Senior Biologist/Executive Director, Loon Preservation Committee

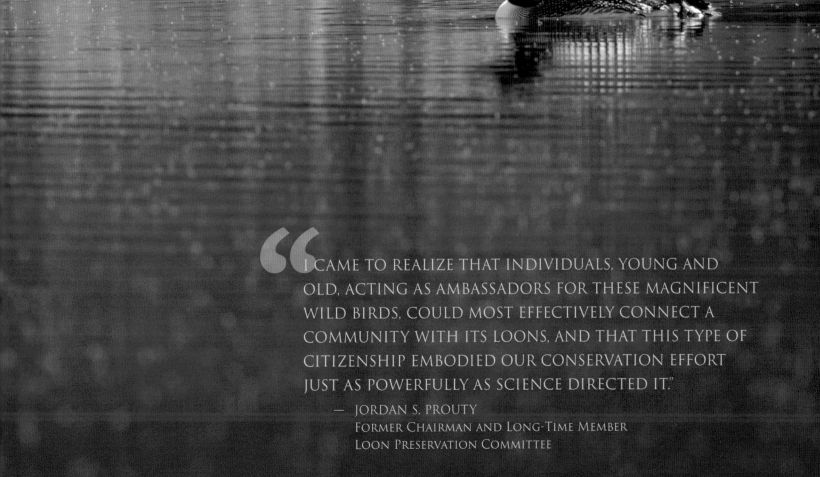

"I CAME TO REALIZE THAT INDIVIDUALS, YOUNG AND OLD, ACTING AS AMBASSADORS FOR THESE MAGNIFICENT WILD BIRDS, COULD MOST EFFECTIVELY CONNECT A COMMUNITY WITH ITS LOONS, AND THAT THIS TYPE OF CITIZENSHIP EMBODIED OUR CONSERVATION EFFORT JUST AS POWERFULLY AS SCIENCE DIRECTED IT."

— JORDAN S. PROUTY
FORMER CHAIRMAN AND LONG-TIME MEMBER
LOON PRESERVATION COMMITTEE

"WHATEVER HAPPENS IN CONSERVATION
IS GOING TO AFFECT THE WHOLE HUMAN
RACE, SO WE ARE ALL GOING TO HAVE TO
PITCH IN AND PLAY OUR PART."
— JOE RICKETTS
Founder, Ricketts Conservation Foundation

Making a Difference: Shifting Conservation Trends

Theodore Roosevelt signed into effect the Antiquities Act of 1906, which allows the President to preserve certain valuable public lands as park and conservation areas. During his tenure, Roosevelt created five national parks, 18 national monuments, 51 federal bird sanctuaries, four national refuges, and designated more than 100 million acres of national forest lands. Thanks to the foresight and legacy of President Roosevelt, the United States government has protected many wild places, securing habitat for species that are uniquely found in those natural areas.

However, governmental agencies have fewer and more limited resources in proportion to the ecological changes and stressors we face in today's world. As a result, a paradigm shift is underway in how wildlife conservation is funded. Government agencies that have been entrusted with the welfare of our wildlife and wilderness areas are increasingly dependent on resources from individuals and private organizations for work that traditionally has been funded by federal and state agencies.

Supported by a generous grant from the Ricketts Conservation Foundation (RCF), Biodiversity Research Institute (BRI) and RCF have initiated the largest and most comprehensive conservation study for the Common Loon, *Restore the Call*. The scope and vision of the RCF-BRI restoration effort is made possible through partnership between private funders and scientists—at a time critical for loons.

In the United States, breeding Common Loons historically nested further south of their current breeding range, including California, Illinois, Indiana, Iowa, Ohio, Oregon, and Pennsylvania. Dedicated conservation efforts in the 1970s, such as those conducted by the Loon Preservation Committee in New Hampshire, have worked to restore loon populations to healthier levels in parts of the Northeast and the Great Lakes Region. Yet, in other states including Idaho, Michigan, North Dakota, Washington, and Wyoming, loon populations remain small or even in decline,

The *Restore the Call* initiative will, for the first time, allow biologists from federal, state, nonprofit, and private organizations to examine and address current threats to loon populations across the United States. This broad and comprehensive approach will most effectively create solutions that strengthen and restore loon populations to their former breeding range.

HOW MANY LOONS?

Estimating the number of Common Loons distributed across their wide and sometimes remote North American range is a challenge. However, through detailed surveys and projections by professional biologists by geographic region—states, provinces, and countries—a reasonable estimate can be developed.

Region	Number of Territorial Pairs	Population Trend
Alaska	4,800	Stable
Idaho	1	Stable
Maine	1,700	Stable
Massachusetts	36	Stable
Michigan	600	Decreasing
Minnesota	4,650	Stable
Montana	72	Increasing
New Hampshire	285	Increasing
New York	243	Increasing
North Dakota	14	Decreasing
Vermont	103	Increasing
Washington	14	Stable
Wisconsin	1,250	Increasing
Wyoming	14	Decreasing
UNITED STATES	**13,782**	Stable

Region	Number of Territorial Pairs	Population Trend
Alberta	1,000	Stable
British Columbia	25,000	Stable
Manitoba	11,000	Stable
New Brunswick	1,100	Decreasing
Newfoundland	5,000	Stable
Northwest Territories	45,000	Stable
Nova Scotia	1,200	Decreasing
Nunavut	5,000	Stable
Ontario	97,000	Decreasing
Quebec	50,000	Decreasing
Saskatchewan	1,750	Stable
Yukon	200	Stable
CANADA	**243,250**	Decreasing
ICELAND	300	Stable
GREENLAND	1,000	Stable
TOTAL POPULATION	**258,332**	Decreasing

The unit most commonly used for tracking loon populations is the number of territorial breeding pairs. Most breeding loons are found in Canada; less than six percent of the population is found in the United States. While populations of Common Loons remain relatively large, significant declines have been documented across the core of their Canadian range over the past two decades. Close monitoring continues to be necessary.

◄—► = Stable   ▲ = Increasing   ▼ = Decreasing

" I LIKE TO REMEMBER THAT WE ARE NOT HERE
FOREVER, AND NOT HERE ALONE, AND THAT THE
RESPECT WITH WHICH WE BEHOLD THE WILD
WORLD MATTERS, IF ANYTHING DOES."
— RICK BASS
AUTHOR AND ENVIRONMENTALIST

RESOURCES FOR MORE INFORMATION

Biodiversity Research Institute's (BRI) Center for Loon Conservation is dedicated toward a greater awareness of loon species worldwide through monitoring, research, and conservation. The Center continues to identify threats to loon populations and develop collaborative research projects to help at-risk populations achieve self-sustaining levels. Supported by a generous grant from the Ricketts Conservation Foundation (RCF), BRI and RCF have initiated the largest and most comprehensive conservation study for the Common Loon, *Restore the Call*.

» www.briloon.org/looncenter/restore
» www.joericketts.com

Other organizations conducting research and monitoring loons include:

Alaska
Alaska Loon and Grebe Watch Monitoring Program »
www.aknhp.uaa.alaska.edu

Maine
Maine Audubon Society » www.maineaudubon.org
Northeast Loon Study Working Group » www.briloon.org/NELSWG

Massachusetts
Department of Conservation and Recreation » www.mass.gov/dcr
The Massachusetts Division of Fisheries and Wildlife (MassWildlife) »
www.mass.gov
Tufts University Wildlife Clinic » www.tufts.edu

Michigan
Common Coast Research and Conservation » www.commoncoast.org
Michigan Loon Preservation Association » www.michiganloons.com
Whitefish Point Bird Observatory » www.wpbo.org

Minnesota
Minnesota Department of Natural Resources » www.dnr.state.mn.us

Montana
Montana Loon Society » www.montanaloons.org
Montana Loon Working Group » www.fwp.mt.gov/fishAndWildlife

New Hampshire
   Loon Preservation Committee » www.loon.org

New York
   BRI's Adirondack Center for Loon Conservation » www.briloon.org/adkloon
   Wildlife Conservation Society » www.wcs.org

Vermont
   Vermont Center for Ecostudies » www.vtecostudies.org

Washington
   Loon Lake Loon Association » www.loons.org

Wisconsin
   Sigurd Olsen Environmental Institute, LoonWatch » www.northland.edu
   The Loon Project » www.loonproject.org
   U.S. Geological Survey: Upper Midwest Environmental Sciences Center »
      www.umesc.usgs.gov
   Wisconsin Department of Natural Resources » www.dnr.wi.gov

Wyoming
   Wyoming Game and Fish Department » http://wgfd.wyo.gov

Canada
   Bird Studies Canada, Canadian Lakes Loon Survey » www.bsc-eoc.org

Packaged with the book is a DVD that features unique video footage gathered by Biodiversity Research Institute and others. Follow the loons through the cycle of seasons, from spring arrival, raising chicks in the summer, fall migration and finally, a return to the sea.

JOURNEY WITH THE
LOON

DVD